It's My STATE!

NEW YORK

The Empire State

Rachel Keranen, Dan Elish, and Stephanie Fitzgerald

Cavendish Square

New York

Published in 2019 by Cavendish Square Publishing, LLC
243 5th Avenue, Suite 136, New York, NY 10016

Fourth Edition

Website: cavendishsq.com

This publication represents the opinions and views of the author based on his or her personal experience, knowledge, and research. The information in this book serves as a general guide only. The author and publisher have used their best efforts in preparing this book and disclaim liability rising directly or indirectly from the use and application of this book.

All websites were available and accurate when this book was sent to press.

Library of Congress Cataloging-in-Publication Data

Names: Keranen, Rachel, author. | Elish, Dan, author. | Fitzgerald, Stephanie, author.
Title: New York : the Empire State / Rachel Keranen, Dan Elish, and Stephanie Fitzgerald.
Description: Fourth edition. | New York : Cavendish Square, [2019] | Series: It's my state! |
"Introduction: The Empire State -- Geography -- The history of New York? --
At work in New York -- State and local government." |
Includes bibliographical references and index. | Audience: Grades 3-5.
Identifiers: LCCN 2017048034 (print) | LCCN 2018000860 (ebook) |
ISBN 9781502626226 (ebook) | ISBN 9781502626240 (library bound) ISBN 9781502644398 (pbk.)
Subjects: LCSH: New York (State)--Juvenile literature. | New York (State)--History--Juvenile literature.
Classification: LCC F119.3 (ebook) | LCC F119.3 .E37 2019 (print) | DDC 974.7--dc23
LC record available at https://lccn.loc.gov/2017048034

Editorial Director: David McNamara
Editor: Caitlyn Miller
Copy Editor: Nathan Heidelberger
Associate Art Director: Alan Sliwinski
Designer: Jessica Nevins
Production Coordinator: Karol Szymczuk
Photo Research: J8 Media

The photographs in this book are used by permission and through the courtesy of: Cover, Francois Roux/Shutterstock.com; p. 4 (top) Lima Junior/Shutterstock.com; (bottom) NY State Flag TK; p. 5; Kristine Paulus (https://www.flickr.com/people/13796250@N00)/Wikimedia Commons/File: Acer saccharum (sugar maple)(10656892444).jpg/CCA 2.0 Generic; p. 6 (top) Ken Thomas/Wikimedia Commons/File: Eastern Bluebird-27527-2.jpg/Public Domain; (bottom) Oleksandr Lytvynenko/Shutterstock.com; p. 7 (top) Jeff Feverston/Shutterstock.com; (bottom) Breck B. Kent/Shutterstock.com; p. 8 Ruth E. Smith/Shutterstock.com; p. 10 (top to bottom) Songquan Deng/Shutterstock.com; European Space Agency/Wikimedia Commons/File: The Great Lakes of North America ESA232155.jpg/CCA-SA 3.0 IGO; Globe Turner/Shutterstock.com; p. 11 Sue Smith/Shutterstock.com; p. 12 Unknown/Wikimedia Commons/File: Half Moon in Hudson.jpg/Public Domain; pp. 13, 15 (L) Rainer Lesniewski/Shutterstock.com; p. 14 Jaro Nemčok (http://nemcok.sk/?contact=3)/Wikimedia Commons/File: Kaaterskill Clove 2016.jpg/CCA-SA 4.0 International; p. 15 (R top) Patrick Nouhailler's (http://www.panoramio.com/user/1286122?with_photo_id=85847601)/Wikimedia Commons/File: From Murray Hill to Sutton Place - panoramio (12).jpg/CCA-SA 3.0 Unported; (R bottom) Marc Venema/Shutterstock.com; p. 16 (top) Alan Tan Photography/Shutterstock.com; (bottom) Littleny/Shutterstock.com; pp. 18 Luciano Mortula LGM/Shutterstock.com; p. 19 (top) Debra Millet/Shutterstock.com; (bottom) Jiawangkun/ Shutterstock.com; pp. 20, 41 Haveseen/Shutterstock.com; p. 21(L) LuckyPhotographer/Shutterstock.com; (R) napattorn686/Shutterstock.com; p. 22 (top) Iofoto/Shutterstock.com; (bottom) Andrea Catenaro/Shutterstock.com; p. 23 Stubblefield Photography/Shutterstock.com; p. 24 Hulton Archive/Getty Images; pp. 26, 27, 28 North Wind Picture Archives; p. 31 (top) Sean Donohue Photo/Shutterstock.com; (bottom) http://www.the-athenaeum.org/art/display_image.php?id=35023/Wikimedia Commons/File: Thomas Birch Commodore Perry Leaving the Lawrence for the Niagara at the Battle of Lake Erie.jpg/Public Domain; p. 32 Kean Collection/Getty Images; p. 33 Fouad A. Saad/Shutterstock.com; pp. 34, 35, 44, (top) 45 Everett Historical/Shutterstock.com; p. 37 Elias Goldensky (1868-1943)/ Library of Congress/Wikimedia Commons/File: FDR in 1933.jpg/Public Domain; p. 38 Gary718/Shutterstock.com; p. 40 Anthony Correia/ Shutterstock.com; p. 44 (bottom) Hugo van Gelderen/Anefo/Wikimedia Commons/File: John Coltrane 1963.jpg/CCA-SA 3.0 Netherlands; p. 46 Melanie Stetson Freeman/The Christian Science Monitor/Getty Images; p. 48 Gleason's Pictorial Drawing-Room Companion, Vol. 2 (January-June, 1852) Boston/Wikimedia Commons/File: Castle Garden, from the Hudson River.tiff/Public Domain; p. 49 (top to bottom) Littleny/ Shutterstock.com; Jim.Henderson/Wikimedia Commons/File: Hunter 68 skyway jeh.jpg/ CC0 1.0 Universal Public Domain Dedication; sach1tb/ Wikimedia Commons/File: Cornell University, Ho Plaza and Sage Hall.jpg/CCA-SA 2.0 Generic; p. 50 Atsushi Hirao/Shutterstock.com; p. 51 Iofoto/Shutterstock.com; p. 52 (top) Dennis W Donohue/Shutterstock.com (bottom) JonathanCollins/Shutterstock.com; p. 53 (top to bottom) Featureflash Photo Agency/Shutterstock.com; Leonard Zhukovsky/Shutterstock.com; Tinseltown/Shutterstock.com; Ga Fullner/Shutterstock. com; p. 55 André Koehne/Wikimedia Commons/File: New York Counties.svg/CCA-SA 3.0 Unported; p. 56 Hramovnick/Shutterstock.com; p. 58 (top) Kathleen Conklin (http://flickr.com/photos/79865753@N00)/Wikimedia Commons /File: Lock on the Cayuga-Seneca Canal.jpg/CCA 2.0 Generic; (bottom) Famartin/Wikimedia Commons/File: 2015-08-20 13 20 10 "Welcome to New York" and "Governor Thomas E Dewey Thruway" signs along northbound Interstate 287 and State Route 17 entering Hillburn, NY from Mahwah, NJ.jpg/CCA-SA 4.0 International; p. 59 (top) BravoKiloVideo/Shutterstock.com; (bottom) Carol Bell/Shutterstock.com; p. 60 (top) Published by B. C. Forbes Publishing Company, NY, 1917/Wikimedia Commons/File: George Eastman 7.jpg/Public Domain; (bottom) Jarek Tuszyński/Wikimedia Commons/File: Kodak No. 1A Autographic Camera - 1.jpg./CCA-SA 4.0 International; p. 61 Bart Sadowski/Shutterstock.com; p. 62 (top to bottom) ItzaVU/Shutterstock. com; Danski14/Wikimedia Commons/File: Hyde collection.jpg/CCA-SA 3.0 Unported; Daderot/Wikimedia Commons/File: Vanderbilt Mansion - IMG 7943.jpg/Public Domain; p. 63 (top) Richard A. McGuirk/Shutterstock.com; (bottom)David Goodfellow/Shutterstock.com; p. 64 Cvrestan/Shutterstock.com; p. 66 Jiawangkun/Getty Images; p. 68 (top) Ritu Manoj Jethani/Shutterstock.com; (bottom) Lee Snider Photo Images/Shutterstock.com p. 69 Mohammed Elshamy/Anadolu Agency/Getty Images; p. 70 Nagel Photography/Shutterstock.com; p. 71 DW labs Incorporated/Shutterstock.com; p. 72 A Katz/ Shutterstock.com

Printed in the United States of America

It's My STATE!

Table of Contents

SNAPSHOT
NEW YORK

The Empire State

Statehood

July 26, 1788

Population

19,849,399
(2017 census estimate)

Capital

Albany

State Flag

The New York State flag is the state seal of New York.

State Seal

The state seal features the state's coat of arms. The shield shows the sun rising over a grassy shore and mountains. Ships sail on the Hudson River, symbolizing trade and business. To the left, Liberty stands with a crown by her left foot, which represents freedom from England. To the right stands Justice, wearing a blindfold. She holds a sword and carries the scales of justice. The state motto, "Excelsior," is written on the white ribbon that flows beneath their feet. "Excelsior" translates to "ever upward." Above the shield, an American eagle sits on a globe.

State Song

New York's state song is "I Love New York" by Steve Karmen. The song's lyrics are an ode to the unique nature of New York: "New York is special. New York is diff'rent ... That's why I love New York!"

HISTORICAL EVENTS TIMELINE

1570–1600

Five Native American tribes (the Mohawk, Oneida, Onondaga, Cayuga, and Seneca) form the Iroquois **Confederacy**.

1609

Henry Hudson explores the Hudson River and claims New York as a colony of the Netherlands.

1664

The English fleet sails into New York harbor. Governor Peter Stuyvesant surrenders without a fight.

State Fruit
Apple

State Flower
Rose

New York started the state flower movement in the late 1800s. Yet the rose was not officially picked as New York's state flower until 1955. This beautiful and **fragrant** flower has more than 150 species. It seems like a fitting choice to represent such a **diverse** state.

State Snack
Yogurt

In 2014, Governor Andrew Cuomo signed a law naming yogurt as New York's state snack. It's a fitting selection because New York makes the most yogurt of any state. New York even produces more Greek yogurt than the country of Greece! Many yogurt companies call New York home, including Chobani and Fage USA.

State Beverage
Milk

1669
The colony is fully in English control. It is renamed New York after James, the Duke of York (King James II).

1825
Erie Canal construction is completed. The canal creates an east-to-west route through New York from the Atlantic to the Great Lakes.

1848
The Seneca Falls women's rights **convention** is held.

State Tree
Sugar Maple

Known best for producing the sap that makes maple syrup, the sugar maple is also one of the world's most beautiful trees. Each fall, its changing leaves paint the New York landscape in brilliant shades of gold, orange, and red.

State Bird
Eastern Bluebird

State Animal
Beaver

2001
Al-Qaeda terrorists fly planes into the World Trade Center, killing about 2,750 in New York. It is the deadliest terror attack in the United States.

2008
David Paterson becomes governor of New York. He is the state's first African American governor and the state's first legally blind governor.

2009
Hillary Clinton, United States senator from New York, is sworn in as secretary of state to President Barack Obama.

State Fish
Brook Trout

Found in the lakes of the Adirondack Mountains, as well as in hundreds of streams throughout the state, the brook trout was named New York's freshwater fish in 1975.

State Fossil

Eurypterus remipes

CURRENT EVENTS TIMELINE

2012
Superstorm Sandy hits New York City and causes widespread damage. The New York Stock Exchange closes for two days.

2014
Baseball star Derek Jeter retires from Major League Baseball. He had played for the New York Yankees for more than twenty years.

2018
Governor Andrew Cuomo unveils a plan to invest $90 million to improve New York's parks and historic landmarks.

This lighthouse casts its light over Lake Ontario, one of
two Great Lakes that New York borders.

1 Geography

New York is a place of contrasts. It borders the Atlantic Ocean, and it also borders the Great Lakes. It has a city of nearly nine million people. Yet there are also vast forests, mountains, and river valleys. It contains the center of finance in the United States. On the other hand, it also produces an abundance of dairy, apples, and other agricultural products.

Ask anyone from outside of the United States what they know about America. Chances are they will mention New York City. The city is a big part of New York State. However, the rest of the state has a wealth of history and culture worth exploring too.

How Glaciers Formed New York

It is hard to imagine that New York's landscape was formed ten thousand to twenty thousand years ago. In fact, it was formed then during

FAST FACT
New York is the only state in America to touch both an ocean (the Atlantic) and a Great Lake (Erie and Ontario). This creates two very different types of coastal regions in one state.

The Laurentide Ice Sheet was taller than many of the skyscrapers in this photo.

Lake Huron (*left*), Lake Erie (*bottom*), and Lake Ontario (*right*) after a snow storm. The Great Lakes are sometimes called "gifts of the glaciers" because they formed in holes that glaciers left behind.

North America's last ice age. The ice age began about one hundred thousand years ago. What is known as the Laurentide Ice Sheet advanced as far as New York. That was about eighteen thousand to twenty-two thousand years ago. This huge glacier towered higher than the Empire State Building and moved across the state. The glacier carved out the Finger Lakes, the Hudson and Mohawk River valleys, and the valleys of the Adirondacks. It also created parts of Long Island. Then, eighteen thousand years ago, the glacier began to melt and its work was revealed.

New York State borders Canada and five US states: Pennsylvania, New Jersey, Connecticut, Massachusetts, and Vermont.

A Closer Look at the Regions of New York

At 54,556 square miles (141,300 square kilometers), New York is the twenty-seventh largest state in area. New York has distinctly different geographic regions. Hugging the Saint Lawrence River in the northeastern section of the state are the flat plains and low hills of the Saint Lawrence Lowland. Also in the northeastern part of the state, the majestic Adirondack Mountains rise. Their region is called the Adirondack Upland. This is wonderful outdoors country. There New Yorkers can visit any of more than three thousand lakes and 30,000 miles (48,280 kilometers) of rivers and streams. Or they can go skiing at one of the area's famous resorts, such as Lake Placid or Gore Mountain. The highlight of a visit would include seeing Mount Marcy. At 5,344 feet (1,629 meters), it is New York's highest peak.

The Adirondack Mountains offer something for everyone: hiking, swimming in lakes, and looking at fall foliage are a few popular activities.

South of the Adirondacks lies the Hudson-Mohawk Lowland. This region contains some of the most fertile farmland in the country. The Hudson and Mohawk Rivers flow through the area. The New England Upland sits to the east of the Hudson River along the Taconic Mountains. The Atlantic Coastal Plain stretches across the southeastern section of the state. This region includes Long Island and the state's beachfront areas along Long Island Sound and the Atlantic Ocean.

The Appalachian Plateau is the largest of the Empire State's geographic regions. It includes the Finger Lakes, the Catskill Mountains, and the Delaware River basin. Known for its flat expanses and beautiful snowy winters, this region has small towns and dairy farms but few cities.

The Erie-Ontario Lowlands region fills most of the northwestern section of the state. This is where Oneida Lake is found as well as three

FAST FACT

Niagara Falls actually consists of three waterfalls that sit on the border of New York and Ontario, Canada. Together, the three waterfalls produce the highest flow rate of any waterfall in the world.

Charting New York

In September 1609, English captain Henry Hudson sailed the *Half Moon* into the Hudson River from the Atlantic Ocean. He was exploring for the Dutch East India Company. Hudson's goal was to find a passage connecting the Atlantic to the Pacific. The company conducted business in present-day Indonesia. They needed a *much* faster way to get there than sailing east around Africa.

Hudson's first mate, Robert Juet, kept a daily journal describing the *Half Moon*'s progress. In 2006, the journal was transcribed by Professor Brea Barthel for an exhibit at the New Netherland Museum. It teaches us a lot about the voyage. Juet observed the region's plants, animals, people, and geography. These observations are seen in the following note from September 14, 1609. (Juet's journal is written in an old form of English. Writing in this form of English used *v*'s at the beginning of words such as "up" and *u*'s in the middle of words such as "river.")

> The fourteenth, in the morning being very faire weather, the wind South-east, we sayled vp the Riuer twelue leagues ... The Riuer is a mile broad: there is very high Land on both sides ... The Land grew very high and Mountainous. The Riuer is full of fish.

An illustration of the *Half Moon*

At this point, the *Half Moon* was in a wide stretch of the Hudson River near Nyack. Hudson thought the widening suggested they were approaching another ocean. But he was wrong. The *Half Moon* sailed up to Albany before the river became too shallow to continue.

The Dutch claimed the region of New York (calling it New Netherland). They later gave it up to the English.

In 1764, King George III of England declared the Connecticut River to be the border between New York and New Hampshire. In 1777, Vermont declared independence from New York, creating part of New York's eastern border.

New York and Connecticut had a series of fights over borders. The 1650 Treaty of Hartford set a border between New Netherland and Connecticut. This border was along a line with one endpoint at Oyster Bay in Long Island. The border moved several times until 1731. The 1731 agreement created the Connecticut Panhandle, a small part of Connecticut that juts into New York. Many people living in this area considered themselves to be part of Connecticut, which is why the panhandle was created. In return, New York gained a narrow sliver of land along the previous New York–Connecticut border.

New York is bounded in part by the Atlantic Ocean in the southeast, Lake Erie and Lake Ontario in the west, and the Saint Lawrence River to the northwest. Much of the northeastern border is created by Lake Champlain. The lake separates New York from Vermont. The eastern border with Massachusetts is created by the Berkshire Mountains.

The Connecticut Panhandle is visible in this map, just north of Long Island.

The Catskill Mountains are especially popular for winter sports.

of the state's major cities: Syracuse, Rochester, and Buffalo. The beautiful coasts of Lakes Erie and Ontario are also in this region. So is one of the most astounding natural wonders in all of America: Niagara Falls.

A Tale of Five Boroughs

Located in the southeastern corner of the state is New York City. New York City is otherwise known as the Big Apple. The city is a collection of five boroughs: the Bronx, Brooklyn, Manhattan, Queens, and Staten Island. These boroughs are partly on the mainland and partly on islands in or facing New York Harbor. They are connected by roads, bridges, ferries, and tunnels.

The island of Manhattan is 13.4 miles (21.6 km) long and 2.3 miles (3.7 km) wide at its widest point. It is only 0.8 miles (1.3 km) wide at its narrowest point. Manhattan is where you can find many famous sites. These include Wall Street and the Financial District, the Empire State Building and many other skyscrapers, Central Park, and the glittering lights of Times Square. A 16-mile (26 km) strait known as the East River separates Manhattan from Brooklyn and Queens, which are on the western end of Long Island.

Brooklyn is the most **populous** and second-largest borough. An estimated 2.7 million people live there. Brooklyn is known for its many diverse and ethnic neighborhoods. Brighton Beach has a large Ukrainian and Russian population. Bedford-Stuyvesant is known for its large African American population. Other neighborhoods include:
- Bensonhurst (traditionally an Italian neighborhood)
- Williamsburg (traditionally Jewish)
- Bushwick (traditionally Puerto Rican)

Some attractions in Brooklyn include Prospect Park, the Brooklyn Botanic Garden, and Coney Island.

Queens is the largest and the second most populous borough. Like Brooklyn, Queens has many neighborhoods that have large ethnic communities. Howard Beach is largely Italian American. Flushing has a large Asian community. Astoria has a large Greek population.

Queens is home to Citi Field (where the New York Mets play), JFK and LaGuardia Airports, and the USTA Billie Jean King National Tennis Center. The US Open tennis tournament is held there every year.

The Bronx is located across the Harlem River from Manhattan. It is the only borough actually located on the US mainland. At 42 square miles (109 sq km), it is the fourth-largest borough. The Bronx was once a rural area. Over time, the addition of subway stations and urban sprawl caused population growth there. Yankee Stadium and the Bronx Zoo are two major attractions in the Bronx. Pelham Bay Park, the largest park in New York City, is also located there. Pelham Bay Park is three times the size of Manhattan's Central Park.

Staten Island lies across Upper New York Bay. It is just a short ferry ride from Lower Manhattan. Staten Island is the third-largest and the least populous borough. Staten Island is mostly residential and industrial. However, the

The five boroughs of New York City

A busy street in Manhattan

The Empire State Building

Citi Field has seats for more than forty thousand baseball fans.

Six hundred species call the Bronx Zoo home.

second-largest park in New York City is being built there. Freshkills Park was once the world's largest landfill. But when it is finished in 2036, the park will feature about 2,200 acres (890 hectares) of trails, waterways, and open land.

Besides New York City's five boroughs, the state has fifty-seven other counties. Therefore, New York has a total of sixty-two counties.

Hot Summers, Snowy Winters

New York State has an extremely varied climate. The people of Western New York, from Syracuse through Rochester and Buffalo, experience harsh winters like those of Canada to the north. More than 100 inches (254 centimeters) of snow can fall each winter. It is not uncommon to have 1 to 3 inches (2.5 to 7.6 cm) of snow fall daily in these areas. But the largest snowfall is due to what is called lake-effect snow.

Lake-effect snow is produced when cold winds move across the warmer waters of Lake Erie and Lake Ontario. The lower layer of air warms and picks up water vapor from the lakes. The water vapor rises through the colder upper layers. It then forms into clouds and is deposited in narrow bands of precipitation. These bands of precipitation slowly move across the region near the lakes. Many inches of snow can fall within hours. When that happens, travel is dangerous.

Syracuse is often ranked the number-one snowiest large city in the United States. Average snowfall there is around 123.8 inches (314 cm). The snowiest winter in Syracuse was the 1992–1993 season. During that season, 192 inches (488 cm) of snow fell. This was due in part to the Blizzard of 1993. Syracuse received 42 inches (107 cm) of snow in two days during this blizzard.

Smaller towns north of Syracuse, however, get even more snow. Over a ten-day period in February 2007, 141 inches (358 cm) of lake-effect snow fell in Redfield, in Oswego County. That is almost 12 feet (3.7 m) of snow!

Not that winter is a picnic for those New Yorkers who live farther south and east. Residents of New York City spend a lot of time commuting outside. That means they must travel during the winter as well. Compared to other parts of the state, the city's weather is tame. New York City averages only around 29 inches (74 cm) of snow a year. However, it is still very cold, and travel can be unpleasant.

What about the Adirondacks? The temperature in the winter can reach into the negative digits. The wind chill often makes the temperature feel even colder. Average snowfall is 103 inches (262 cm) in Lake Placid during the winter. Skiers and other winter-sports enthusiasts love the Adirondacks because of its cold and snowy weather.

Of course, New York does have more temperate seasons. In fact, New Yorkers experience the full effect of all four seasons. Autumn is one of the most celebrated seasons. The crisp autumn air comes to the state in September. It generally lingers into early November. This is the time to witness the incredible fall foliage for which New York and other northeastern states are famous. The state is located far enough south that spring comes relatively early. Moderate temperatures then last through June. Beautiful spring blossoms can be seen everywhere. Summers, too, can be extremely pleasant. But sometimes they are also quite hot. Especially in the lower portions of the state, July and August daytime temperatures can reach the upper 90s Fahrenheit (upper 30s Celsius).

New York's Biggest Cities

(Population numbers are from the US Census Bureau's 2017 projections for incorporated cities.)

Times Square in New York City

1. New York City: population 8,622,698 people

New York City is the most populated city in the United States. The number of people who live in New York City makes up 43 percent of the entire state's population!

2. Buffalo: population 258,612

Buffalo, in Western New York, is known for its cold and snowy winters. It is where buffalo chicken wings were invented. Buffalo is home to a wealth of architectural treasures, including buildings designed by Frank Lloyd Wright and Louis Sullivan.

3. Rochester: population 208,046

Rochester has a rich music and arts culture. It is home to the Eastman School of Music, the George Eastman Museum dedicated to photography and film, and the Memorial Art Gallery.

4. Yonkers: population 202,019

Many people think Yonkers is the sixth borough of New York City because it is only a few miles north. Yonkers is home to the Hudson River Museum.

5. Syracuse: population 143,396

Nicknamed "The Salt City," Syracuse was the largest producer of salt in the United States in the 1800s. Once the Erie Canal was completed, it provided a route to ship the salt across the state and beyond. This helped Syracuse grow.

6. Albany: population 98,251

Albany became New York's state capital in 1797. After the Erie Canal was built, Albany became an important port city because of its location. Goods from the Midwest could easily reach New York

Syracuse

City, and vice versa. Today, residents and visitors enjoy the city's entertainment venues, parks, and its nearness to mountain ranges.

7. New Rochelle: population 79,946

New Rochelle, located just northeast of New York City, was settled by Huguenots (French protestants) fleeing religious **persecution** in France in the late 1600s. Many of the refugees were from the French town of La Rochelle.

8. Mount Vernon: population 68,703

Mount Vernon is just north of the Bronx. In 1894, Mount Vernon and Yonkers residents voted to stay separate from New York City.

9. Schenectady: population 65,625

Schenectady, located about 20 miles (32 km) west of Albany, is often called "The City That Lights and Hauls the World." This is because GE Power, a division of General Electric, is based out of the city. Additionally, Schenectady once featured a now-closed locomotive company.

10. Utica: population 60,635

After the completion of the Erie Canal, Utica became a stopping point for travelers. By the mid-1800s, Utica grew into a small city with many businesses.

Utica

Letchworth State Park, south of Rochester, is a great place to watch the seasons change.

New York's Wildlife

Much has changed in New York State over the past four hundred years. When settlers first arrived, the region was covered from end to end with forests and meadows. Today, cities, towns, factories, and farms cover much of the land.

Not everything has changed, however. Around 63 percent of the state remains forested. There are still plenty of wild places to be found in New York. New York is home to 7,600 freshwater lakes, ponds, and reservoirs. The state also has a portion of two of the Great Lakes. More than 70,000 miles (112,650 km) of rivers and streams flow through the state. The vast forests are home to many hundreds of different kinds of wildlife.

New York has set aside some wonderful places to see all this spectacular wildlife. Among other things, you can look for moose in the Adirondack Mountains. You can visit the southeastern shore of Lake Ontario to watch raptors make their spring migration. Or you can track deer on Fire Island (a barrier island off the south shore of Long Island).

New York's animals are managed and protected by a state government agency called the Bureau of Wildlife. It was founded by the state **legislature** in 1895. Because of its efforts, species such as the beaver, white-tailed deer, wood duck, bald eagle, and peregrine falcon have been brought back from the brink of extinction.

New York's Diverse Offerings

New York's diverse geography and rich natural resources provide bountiful opportunities. These include fresh food to eat from the land and the sea, mountain recreation, and days at the beach. Its distinct four seasons add to the many options.

Niagara Falls and Other Top Attractions

Each year, millions visit Niagara Falls USA to take in the stunning natural beauty of the falls. Estimates from 2015 put the number of monthly visitors to Niagara Falls USA at more than six hundred thousand people. Tourists can enjoy guided hikes at state parks, an aquarium, a nature center, and more. Seasonal attractions include fireworks on the Fourth of July and a special slate of activities for the holidays.

According to the Niagara Tourism and Convention Corporation, thanks to the falls, more than 20 percent of people in Niagara County work in the tourism industry.

In addition to Niagara Falls, New York State offers many other outdoor attractions—some, like Central Park, are even in the middle of New York City! Central Park spans 843 acres (341 ha). Every year, forty million people enjoy the park's gardens, lake, and outdoor concert venues.

New York City's wildly popular manmade attractions include the Statue of Liberty, the Empire State Building, and Times Square. In fact, Times Square often ranks as the most-visited attraction in the United States.

Of course, popular tourist attractions can be found throughout the state of New York. Museums, parks, historical sites, and important works of architecture can be found in every region.

The Statue of Liberty was a gift from France.

Summer and fall are the most popular seasons to visit Niagara Falls.

What Lives in New York?

Flora

Beech Trees The American beech is likely the most widely distributed tree in the state. It grows in the Adirondacks and the Catskills as well as the rest of the state. One of the reasons it is so populous is that the wood is not as valuable as some other kinds of trees. This means that American beeches were left to grow while other trees were cut down. An American beech also provides heavy shade cover, which prevents other trees from growing.

American beech tree

Sugar Maples The sugar maple is abundant everywhere in New York except on Long Island. The sugar maple provides the sap needed to make maple syrup. There are thousands of sugar bushes (the name for groves of maple trees) throughout the state. The tree also provides good wood for furniture, flooring, and other purposes.

Eastern White Pine The eastern white pine is one of the most widely distributed pine trees native to New York. It grows on the steep slopes of the Adirondacks as well as in the central and western parts of the state. It is a soft wood and has many uses in woodworking.

Apple Trees New York is the second-biggest apple producing state in the country. Apple production in the state generates more than $300 million in revenue each year. McIntosh is the most widely grown apple in New York, followed by the Empire apple.

An apple orchard on Long Island

Summer Grapes The *Vitis aestivalis* grape species is native to eastern North America. One variety (cultivar) called Norton is the oldest known American grape cultivar used commercially.

Fauna

Beaver The beaver is New York State's official animal. Beavers live in bodies of water including wooded streams, swamps, and marshes, and at the edges of lakes and ponds. They eat tree leaves, bark, and twigs, which New York has plenty of!

Eastern Bluebird The bluebird was made the state bird in 1970. Many people hang special nesting boxes on fences to attract these pretty, sweet-sounding birds, which winter throughout the state.

White-Tailed Deer The white-tailed deer is the most popular animal hunted for meat in New York and can be found throughout the state. They can run up to 40 miles (64.3 km) per hour and leap 8-foot (2.4 m) fences.

Black Bear There are approximately six thousand to eight thousand black bears in New York. Adult males weigh about 300 pounds (136 kilograms). Females weigh about 170 pounds (77 kg). Most black bears live in the Adirondacks and the Catskills. About 10 to 15 percent live in the central-western region of the state.

Red-tailed hawk

Red-Tailed Hawk The red-tailed hawk is likely New York's most common bird of prey. It thrives in New York City. There it has plenty of rats and mice to eat, as well as buildings and bridges to nest on.

Oysters Once, half of the world's oysters came from New York Harbor. In the 1800s, oysters covered the harbor. They filtered the water and reduced erosion on the coast by blunting the force of the waves. Human pollution and activity led to near extinction of oysters in the harbor. The New York City Environmental Protection Department is working to restore the oyster population.

Native Americans from Canada fought in New York alongside British general John Burgoyne during the American Revolution.

2 The History of New York

In 1600, New York was inhabited by many Native American nations, including the Seneca, Cayuga, Onondaga, Oneida, Mohawk, and the Algonquin tribes. Over time, new tribes entered the area. Territories shifted.

The seventeenth century also brought new groups of people from Europe. At the time, European countries were sending explorers around the globe to find valuable resources. Countries in Europe also wanted to claim "new" lands as colonies. The first country to claim present-day New York as a colony was the Netherlands in 1609.

New York's First People

Archaeologists continue to discover spearheads and stone knives left by New York's first Native American residents. However, little is known about them.

The first documented history of the region begins with the Native Americans who were in the area shortly before the arrival of

FAST FACT
Ten thousand years ago, the region that now includes New York State was populated by hunters. They tracked herds of elk and caribou, and caught bears, fish, and small mammals. They also gathered plants and seeds from the forest.

This woodcut shows longhouses on Manhattan Island in the 1500s.

European explorers and settlers. Several tribes of Algonquian-speaking people populated the southeastern part of what is now New York State. This included the Lenape, Montauk, and Mahican tribes. They lived along the banks of the lower Hudson River and on Staten Island, Long Island, and Manhattan.

When Europeans began to arrive, the Algonquian-speaking tribes came into contact with Europeans more frequently than the Iroquois. This contact brought trade. Yet it also caused tensions between the Europeans and Native Americans. **Devastating**, deadly European diseases killed many Native people. Due to this devastation and tension, eventually the Algonquian-speaking tribes disappeared from the area.

Farther upstate lived the Mohawk, Oneida, Onondaga, Cayuga, and Seneca tribes. These tribes called themselves the "people of the longhouse." They were enemies of the Algonquian-speaking tribes and contributed to their departure from New York. They also fought among themselves at times.

Sometime between 1570 and 1600, the five tribes formed a confederation. They called the confederation Haudenosaunee. The Europeans called it the Iroquois Confederacy. This was a political organization in which each tribe enjoyed some independence. However, each tribe answered to the authority of the confederacy's Great Council. The confederation tightened cultural and spiritual bonds. Most important, the tribes agreed to fight together against invaders and not against each other. At the height of its power, the Iroquois Confederacy dominated New York and the Lake Erie region. (In 1722, the Tuscarora tribe joined the confederacy.)

Europeans Arrive

The written history of what is now New York begins in 1524 with Italian explorer Giovanni da Verrazzano. Verrazzano sailed from modern-day North Carolina north to New York Harbor and along Long Island. A group of Native people, likely the Lenape, watched him from the shores of New York Harbor. Verrazzano later described the event as follows: "They came toward us very cheerfully, making great sounds of admiration, showing us where we might come to land most safely with our boat." He also noted what many other new arrivals to New York City throughout the years have thought: "[It] seemed so commodious and delightful, and ... we supposed [it] must also contain great riches."

Though Verrazzano soon sailed back to Europe, other explorers followed in search of those riches. In 1608, Frenchman Samuel de Champlain set up a fur trading post near present-day Quebec, Canada. In 1609, he discovered what is now known as Lake Champlain. Part of this lake lies in the northeastern section of New York State. Also in 1609, explorer Henry Hudson sailed into what is now called New York Harbor. He navigated the river that today bears his name. Hudson traveled as far north as present-day Albany.

The settlement of New Amsterdam

In 1624, the Dutch set up a fur trading post and settlement in what they called Fort Orange (present-day Albany). This was the first permanent European settlement in the region. It was soon followed by the settlement of New Amsterdam at the southern tip of the island of Manhattan.

By the 1660s, there were several Dutch settlements in what is now New York City. On the northern end of Manhattan was a farming

New York's Native People

Long before the first settlers reached New York's shores, Native people had made the region their home. The Algonquian-speaking people, the Haudenosaunee, and other tribes lived across the state. The Lenape lived in the southern part of the state, where New York City is today. Other Algonquian-speaking tribes and the Haudenosaunee lived in Central and Western New York. (The Haudenosaunee were later known as the Iroquois.) The Algonquian-speaking tribes in New York included the Lenape, Mahican, Mohegan, Abenaki, and Poospatuck tribes. Most tribes settled on the different waterways. The Finger Lakes, Lake Champlain, and Lake George were a few.

Each tribe thrived in the untamed wilderness. They had unique governments, religions, and cultures. The cultures of these Native American tribes are important parts of New York's history. These tribes also had many things in common. Most got their food primarily from farming. They also fished, hunted, and gathered. They made their houses from the bark and wood of trees. The Iroquois made long, wood houses called longhouses. The Algonquian-speaking tribes lived in smaller, round houses known as wigwams. They also played games similar to lacrosse and told stories.

When the Europeans arrived in the New York region, they were looking for furs. The Dutch traded with the Algonquian-speaking tribes. The Dutch gave them iron axes, cloth, mirrors, liquor, and other goods in exchange for furs. The Iroquois, meanwhile, traded with the British. The Iroquois exchanged furs for rifles, metal axes, alcohol, and other goods. Guns changed the lives of the Native Americans. They could hunt more easily and were armed with much deadlier weapons when they went to war. There was a large difference in gun ownership between the Algonquian-speaking tribes (who the Dutch sought to keep unarmed) and the Iroquois. It contributed to the downfall of the Algonquian-speaking people.

Guns weren't the only things Europeans introduced. Deadly diseases such as

The first step of building a wigwam is constructing a frame.

smallpox and cholera were brought over from Europe. The Native Americans did not have any resistance to these new diseases. A huge portion of the Native population died.

Today, there are eight federally recognized Native tribes in New York. The Seneca, Cayuga, Oneida, Onondaga, and Tuscarora Nations, as well as the Saint Regis Mohawk Tribe and the Tonawanda Band of Seneca, were all at one point part of the Iroquois Nation. The eighth tribe is the Shinnecock. They are located in Southampton. The tribes have seen huge changes since the Europeans settled in New York. These include a major loss of population and territory. Today, there are just over two hundred thousand Native American people who live in the state.

The Iroquois Confederacy

The Iroquois Confederacy is a group of Native American tribes that lived, and continue to live, in New York State. The tribes were distinct in territory, language, and culture. However, they shared a common linguistic and cultural history. Formed sometime between 1570 and 1600, the confederacy is one of the oldest democracies in the world.

"Iroquois" was a name made up by the French who first encountered the tribes in the seventeenth century. The Iroquois called themselves the Haudenosaunee. "Haudenosaunee" means "People of the Longhouse."

Organization: Iroquois nations are divided into clans. Iroquois clans are families that share a common female ancestor. Each clan was named after an animal. Each clan selected a chief who gathered in a Grand Council of Chiefs to make major decisions that affected the entire confederacy.

Food: In the past, Iroquois women tended the vegetable fields. The three main crops that they grew were known as the Three Sisters: corn, beans, and squash. The Iroquois not only ate these vegetables, but they also used their byproducts to make cooking tools and other useful things. Iroquois men hunted deer, as well as wild turkeys and migratory birds, beavers, and other animals. They also fished during the spring and summer.

Women: Women held a lot of power in the Iroquois Confederacy. Women elected the chiefs and local leaders. Children inherited their mother's status. Clan leaders were the oldest or most respected female in the family.

Fun Facts: Lacrosse's history can be traced back to games that the Iroquois played. Iroquois villages often moved every ten to twenty years to find fresh land for hunting and farming.

community called Nieuw Haarlem (now the neighborhood known as Harlem). Across the East River was Breuckelen (now Brooklyn). Across the Harlem River, a village grew around a farm owned by Jonas Bronck. The area came to be known as Bronck's Land. Later it was renamed the Bronx. The collection of Dutch settlements in and around present-day New York were known as New Netherland.

Before long, events in Europe intruded on the peaceful Dutch community. War broke out between England and the Netherlands. In 1664, English warships sailed into New York Harbor. Dutch governor Peter Stuyvesant saw he was hopelessly outnumbered. He surrendered New Netherland to the English. Soon afterward, King Charles II of England gave the new land to his brother, the duke of York. Much of the former Dutch colony was renamed New York. The English allowed the Dutch settlers to stay. Soon new Dutch, French, German, and English colonists were arriving in New York.

The American Revolution

By the mid-1700s, thirteen colonies of Great Britain stretched along the Atlantic seaboard from Georgia to what is now Maine. From 1754 to 1763, the British and French battled for control of the North American fur trade. In 1763, with the help of the powerful Iroquois, the British won what came to be known as the French and Indian War. The British government had spent a great deal of money fighting the French. To raise money quickly, the British government decided to tax the American colonists. This was a fateful mistake.

Some colonists remained loyal to the British king and Parliament, but many others objected

to paying for Britain's wars. These colonists felt it was unfair that they could be taxed when there was no one representing their interests thousands of miles away in the British Parliament in London. Tensions built. "No taxation

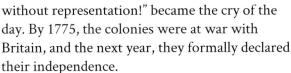
Reenactors commemorate the Battle of Saratoga.

without representation!" became the cry of the day. By 1775, the colonies were at war with Britain, and the next year, they formally declared their independence.

The first shots of the war were fired in Massachusetts, but New York was quickly identified as a **strategic** area. The colony lay between New England and the other colonies farther south. Britain's strategy was to occupy New York in order to split the colonies. As a result, nearly one-third of the war's battles were fought in New York. In 1776, the British occupied New York City. Not long after, in 1777, a very important battle, often called the turning point of the American Revolution, took place near Saratoga, north of Albany. After the British were defeated at the Battle of Saratoga, France decided to join the war on the American side. With French help, the colonist defeated the British and won their independence.

This 1815 painting shows the Battle of Lake Erie during the War of 1812.

After the war was officially over in 1783, the British gave their land to the United States, not their Native American allies. New York State needed to raise money. New York officials bought millions of acres of land in western New York from the Iroquois at a very low price. They then sold the land off to white settlers. Many New Englanders jumped at the chance, and soon new towns called Hudson, Ithaca, Syracuse, and

New York City in 1828

Buffalo sprang up in the western and northern sections of the state. The state of New York kept repeating this practice until the Haudenosaunee had very little land left.

Peace between the Americans and the British did not last for long. From 1812 to 1815, the United States fought another war with Britain. It was called the War of 1812. Parts of New York were turned into battlefields once more. British troops attacked Fort Niagara and destroyed neighboring farms and villages. In a second **raid**, the British burned the settlements in Buffalo. New York was also the scene of Thomas Macdonough's important victory for the American navy in the Battle of Lake Champlain near Plattsburgh. When the war finally ended in 1815, New Yorkers were free to get back to building communities and businesses. By 1820, almost 1.4 million people lived in New York. At that time, it was the most populated state in the country.

New York During the Civil War

In the 1800s, New York's economy was picking up. Yet much of the state's success was built on shaky ground—mainly the institution of slavery. From the time the Dutch occupied the area, there were slaves in New York. The practice of owning slaves in New York continued through the 1700s. Even after slavery was abolished in the state in 1827, some New Yorkers profited from slave labor. New York bankers and merchants lent money to and traded with cotton growers and merchants in the South. These New Yorkers made a great deal of money from the South's cotton industry. It was an industry that depended on slave labor.

Build a Pinhole Camera

George Eastman developed the Kodak camera in Rochester, New York. It was the first camera to make photography accessible to beginner photographers of all ages.

The first photography cameras were modeled after pinhole cameras. Pinhole cameras (also called camera obscuras) were used thousands of years ago. People in ancient China and ancient Egypt used them to study solar eclipses and properties of light.

Make your own pinhole camera and learn how photography works!

Supplies:

- A pushpin or tack
- A cardboard box with a lid or a cardboard canister such as an oatmeal container
- Scissors

- Ruler
- Wax paper
- Tape
- Blanket
- Decorations (optional)

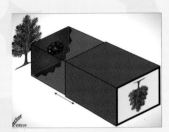

Steps

1. Use the pushpin or tack to poke a tiny hole in one end of the box or canister. (This is the pinhole.)
2. Ask an adult to cut a 2-inch (5 cm) square on the side of the box or canister directly opposite the pinhole poked in Step 1.
3. With the scissors, cut a 3-inch (7.6 cm) square of wax paper.
4. Tape the wax paper square over the square cut-out in the box.
5. Decorate your pinhole camera, if desired.
6. Go into a dark room with a bright light source, such as a lamp. Turn the lamp on and stand several feet away from the light.
7. Drape the blanket over your head and the base of the camera.
8. Aim the pinhole end of the camera at the lamp and, holding the camera at arm's length, look at the wax paper end.
9. You should see an upside-down image in your pinhole camera. All of the incoming light is focused through the small pinhole and hits the wax paper. This is how the glass lens of a camera works. In a camera, the lens allows light to move through the camera. The light hits the film in the back (here, the wax paper). The film is coated with layers of chemicals that respond to the light and form an image.
10. If you want an even more advanced project, visit Kodak's website to find a tutorial about using photographic film in your homemade pinhole camera.

Looters steal from a Brooks Brothers store in New York City during the 1863 draft riots.

By the time the **American Civil War** broke out in 1861, many people in the North (including in New York State) were strongly opposed to slavery. They wanted to see it end. But not everyone was willing to fight for the cause.

President Abraham Lincoln signed the Enrollment Act of 1863, a bill that established a draft into the army. Many citizens were furious. News of the bloody battle at Gettysburg was on the front page of the major papers. Lincoln's call for three hundred thousand more soldiers frightened even those people who believed in the cause. And many poor people were angry that wealthy citizens could buy their way out of service. It cost $300 (nearly $6,000 in today's dollars) to do so.

The result was the New York City draft riots. For four days in July of 1863, mobs swarmed through the city's streets. They protested the war by looting stores and burning buildings. City government buildings and those owned by African Americans were especially targeted. At least 119 people died in the riots. Some think the death total was as many as 500 or 1,000. Union troops had to be pulled from the front lines to help restore order.

Despite the horror of the draft riots, New York State and its citizens ultimately rallied to the Union cause. By the war's end in 1865, New York State had supplied the most troops, money, arms, and food of any Northern state. More than four thousand free blacks from New York served in the

Union army. New York also suffered the greatest casualties of any state. In all, about fifty-three thousand soldiers from New York died.

New Technologies Arise

In the mid-1800s, America entered a period known as the Industrial Revolution. The Industrial Revolution was when new technologies made it easier for industries to produce goods in big factories. Business boomed. Buffalo became the home of many steel plants. Railroad tracks were laid down throughout the state, connecting cities and towns. The first New York City elevated railway—known as the "El"—opened for business in the late 1800s.

At the same time, a new generation of business leaders began to make its mark on American industry. A man from New York named Isaac Singer improved the design of the sewing machine. Soon factories were producing them by the hundreds. Elisha Graves Otis invented the elevator brake. This innovation made the idea of building skyscrapers a reality. He started a company in Yonkers that made electric elevators for high-rise buildings. In Rochester, a bank teller named George Eastman invented and mass-produced the first hand-held camera. John D. Rockefeller, who was born near Ithaca, established the Standard Oil Company. He became one of the richest people in America.

Successful businesses needed a vibrant workforce. Technological advances in industry came at the same time as the first big wave of German and Irish **immigrants** in the mid-1800s. In the late 1800s and early 1900s, they were followed by even larger numbers immigrants. Many of the people in this wave of immigration were Eastern European Jews, Italians, and Greeks. Most of these new Americans found work.

The 1901 Pan-American Exposition was held in Buffalo. It celebrated the advances of the Industrial Revolution.

In 1848, Lucretia
Mott and Elizabeth
Cady Stanton
organized the
nation's first
women's rights
convention in
Seneca Falls, New
York. Nearly two
hundred women
showed up to pass
resolutions calling
for equal rights for
women, including
the right to vote.
The convention
launched the
women's **suffrage**
movement in the
United States.
"Suffrage" means
the right to vote.

However, it was usually in "sweatshops." For most factory workers, the workday was very long. Their pay was very low. Worse, their working conditions were often unsafe and unclean. Even young children worked twelve-hour days. By 1900, huge numbers of immigrants were living in slums, even as the rich grew richer.

New York Booms and Busts

New York raced into the twentieth century with a roar. Until the end of the nineteenth century, "New York City" meant "Manhattan." In 1898, Brooklyn, the Bronx, Queens, and Staten Island officially joined New York City. Their addition increased the city's area more than tenfold and almost doubled its population (to 3.4 million people). Now it was the second-largest city in the world, after London. Business continued to thrive. Soon the New York Stock Exchange on Wall Street was trading millions of dollars' worth of shares a day. The famous Manhattan skyline with rows of skyscrapers began to take shape.

But while industrialists built giant mansions, the slums continued to grow. New York was a state of great wealth and achievement. It was also a place of great poverty and need.

From 1919 to 1920 and again from 1923 to 1928, Al Smith was governor of New York. Among other things, Smith focused on providing better housing and welfare services for New Yorkers. He channeled money into public programs for parks, highways, and bridges. He helped to institute labor laws to protect workers, including children. Despite Smith's great achievements, there was trouble ahead for New York and America.

In 1929, the entire country was hit by the Great Depression. Many people lost their jobs. In 1931, New York governor Franklin Delano Roosevelt created the Temporary Emergency Relief Administration. New York became the first state in the nation to give state aid to the unemployed. After being elected president in 1932, Roosevelt continued where he had left off. He created what he called the New Deal. The New Deal was a series of nationwide public works and social-service programs designed to give aid and jobs to Americans who had been hit hardest by the Depression. Recovery was slow. However, Roosevelt's policies helped New Yorkers dig themselves out of one of the most difficult periods in their history.

Franklin Delano Roosevelt began his political career in New York. In 1933, he became president of the United States.

World War II's Legacy

In 1939, World War II began in Europe. The United States stayed out of the fighting at first. Then Japan bombed the US naval base at Pearl Harbor, Hawaii, in 1941. The nation joined the war. New York State did its share in the massive effort to defeat the governments of Germany, Japan, and Italy. The Brooklyn Navy Yard became the busiest naval shipyard in the world. At peak operations, a ship left New York Harbor for the war every fifteen minutes. More than three million troops and their equipment and 63 million tons (57 million metric tons) of supplies and materials were soon shipped overseas from the Empire State. Peace came in 1945. The entire country, including New York, experienced an enormous economic boom.

Several large manufacturing companies had been established in Upstate New York in the late 1800s and early 1900s. As their businesses grew, so did the need for more workers. Soon African Americans from the South and men and women

The Macy's Thanksgiving Day Parade

Thanksgiving is a national holiday across the United States, but New York City celebrates it in a special way. Each year, the city hosts the Macy's Thanksgiving Day Parade.

The Macy's Thanksgiving Day Parade began in 1924. When it started, it was called the Macy's Christmas Parade. That's because Macy's planned the parade as an event that would get customers excited about shopping for the holiday season. The first Macy's department store was located in Herald Square in Manhattan. Business was booming there and at Macy's stores across the country.

In its first year, the parade featured animals from the Central Park Zoo and floats with characters including Little Miss Muffet and Red Riding Hood. Santa rode at the end of the parade in a sleigh pulled by reindeer. When the parade reached the Macy's department store, Santa was crowned "King of the Kiddies." Then the Macy's Christmas windows were unveiled. The windows were filled with moving characters from Mother Goose.

In 1927, the parade became known as the Thanksgiving Day Parade. This was also the year that the parade began to feature giant balloon characters. They included Felix the Cat, a dinosaur, a caveman, and various animals. Today, the parade contains more than eight thousand participants and dozens of floats and giant balloons. They march about 2.5 miles (4 km) through Manhattan. Each balloon is designed at Macy's by artists called "balloonatics." Santa still brings up the rear of the parade.

It's estimated that 3.5 million New Yorkers watch the parade in person. The parade is free, so many arrive before dawn to claim a spot along the route. (Some people even go to the American Museum of Natural History to watch the inflation of the giant balloons outside of the museum the day before Thanksgiving.) Many people get excited each year to see the traditional balloons again and new balloons for the first time. And approximately 50 million people watch the parade on television. That's almost one-sixth of the country!

Snoopy has appeared in more Macy's Thanksgiving Day Parades than any other mascot or character.

from Puerto Rico poured into the state looking for work. By the 1960s, the racial tension and civil unrest that could be felt around the country bubbled over in New York. On July 18, 1964, riots erupted in Harlem. Less than a week later, on July 24, there were riots in Rochester, prompting a state of emergency. The state's National Guard had to be called in to restore order. This was the first time the National Guard had ever been called in to a northern city.

The Turn of the Twenty-First Century

As the turn of the century neared, New York State experienced an economic slowdown. Good economic times nationwide for most of the 1980s and 1990s helped New Yorkers bounce back. New York's economy shifted. Manufacturing shrunk. Education, health, and social service industries grew.

As the national economy and stock market grew in the 1990s, New York City benefited. Young professionals increasingly saw the city as a desirable place to live and work. Rudolph Giuliani, New York's mayor from 1994 until 2001, also worked to improve the city's image. He successfully reduced crime, which brought more tourists.

Then, on the morning of September 11, 2001, tragedy struck. Terrorists hijacked four airplanes. At 8:46 a.m., the terrorists crashed one of the planes into the top floors of the north tower of the famous World Trade Center's Twin Towers in Manhattan. At 9:03 a.m., a second plane crashed into the south tower. Though some people managed to escape from the burning buildings, many were not so lucky. By the end of the day, both enormous towers had collapsed,

More than three hundred New York firefighters lost their lives helping others on September 11.

and almost 3,000 people were dead. Among them were 60 police officers and 343 firefighters. A third plane was flown into the Pentagon (the US Department of Defense headquarters, outside Washington, DC), killing almost two hundred people. The fourth plane crashed in a field near Pittsburgh, Pennsylvania, killing all forty passengers and crew. The September 11 terrorist attack was the worst terrorist attack ever to occur on American soil.

The destruction of the World Trade Center's Twin Towers was a national tragedy that was particularly devastating for New York City. But out of disaster, New Yorkers bonded as never before and showed the world the unique nature of their strength and spirit. Volunteers rushed downtown to search for survivors and to help clear debris. Others lined up to donate blood and feed the firefighters and other rescue workers who were working at the site. Money poured in to aid families of victims. The incredible bravery of the firefighters and police officers was acknowledged worldwide, as was Mayor Giuliani's skillful leadership during the city's darkest days.

Over time, the citizens of New York got back to business as usual. A 1,776-foot (541 m) skyscraper now stands next to the site of the former World Trade Center's Twin Towers. The site also includes a memorial to the victims and a museum.

One World Trade Center is the tallest building in the Western Hemisphere.

Occupy Wall Street

On July 13, 2011, protesters gathered by the hundreds and set up camp in the Financial District in New York City. These protesters were part of a movement called Occupy Wall Street. The movement started with a blog post published by *Adbusters* magazine that urged Americans to come together and camp out on Wall Street to protest the power and greed of corporations. Two months later, more than one hundred people began to occupy Zuccotti Park, a privately owned public park less than a mile from Wall Street. In addition to camping in the park, protesters marched in the Financial District.

One interesting part of the Occupy Wall Street movement was that the group decided against having a leader. Everyone in the movement worked together to decide their goals. At times, not having a leader led to confusion. Sometimes the group found it difficult to decide on goals. However, the example set by the Occupy Wall Street movement led to similar "Occupy"

movements in other cities, including Los Angeles and Washington, DC. Still, people around the United States were divided on whether or not to support the protesters.

A major complication of Occupy Wall Street was that Zuccotti Park was not designed to house hundreds of people. Officials in New York City wanted to evict (or remove) protesters in order to clean up the park, which over time became filled with trash. Protesters did not want to leave and felt that city officials were trying to silence them. On November 15, 2011, the protesters were evicted from Zuccotti Park at 1:00 a.m. The protesters were told they could return to the park after it was cleaned, but they were no longer allowed to camp there in tents or under tarps.

After the eviction, the movement could not find a way to extend their protest in Zuccotti Park. Occupy Wall Street still exists but does not get as much media attention as they did for those two months in 2011 when they were at their strongest. Today, the movement is credited with bringing attention to important issues.

Buffalo Billion

The Occupy Wall Street movement shows just how important economic issues are to Americans. Of course, protests aren't the only way to achieve change. In January of 2012, Governor Andrew Cuomo announced a new plan to help the economy of Western New York. Called the Buffalo Billion, the plan was designed to give $1 billion to Buffalo, New York, over five years. In January 2017, Cuomo said he intended to add an additional $500 million to the plan.

The Buffalo Billion money has gone toward building high-tech facilities in Buffalo. Software, manufacturing, and medicine are a few industries that have benefited from the investment. Another part of the Buffalo Billion plan helps aspiring homeowners buy houses in Buffalo and helps people who are at risk of foreclosure keep their homes. (Foreclosure is when a bank takes back a house because a homeowner is unable to pay his or her mortgage.)

Leaders hope the Buffalo Billion plan will pay off for the city of Buffalo.

The Buffalo Billion plan is not without its critics, though. Some people feel that the investment was too large. Others feel like the first $1 billion should have been enough and are unsure why Governor Cuomo added another $500 million. These people say that if the plan worked, there would be no need for the extra money. Finally, there has been some corruption linked to the plan. Corruption means that people misuse their power and money, sometimes by taking bribes. However, with a plan as large and ambitious as the Buffalo Billion, it will take many years to decide if the investment paid off.

A Remarkable Past and a Bright Future

In some ways, the history of New York State and New York City represent the entire nation's past. There is little that happens nationally that doesn't happen in New York as well. Maybe that is because the state is so diverse. There's no doubt that New York has shaped and has been shaped by some of the most influential people and events the country has ever seen.

Important New Yorkers

Susan B. Anthony

John Coltrane

Susan B. Anthony

Susan B. Anthony was a women's rights activist and social reformer. She successfully petitioned for women to be admitted to the University of Rochester. She campaigned for women's right to vote and was arrested for voting in Rochester in 1872. She became the first woman to appear on US coinage in 1979.

John Coltrane

John Coltrane was a famous jazz saxophonist. He studied at music schools before joining the US Navy. He played in the US Navy Band in Hawaii. Later, Coltrane formed a quartet famous for songs like his version of "My Favorite Things." He died in 1967 while living on Long Island.

Alexander Hamilton

Alexander Hamilton was born around 1755 in the British West Indies. He became a New York delegate to the Constitutional Convention. He was a major author of the Federalist Papers, which encouraged adoption of the United States Constitution. Hamilton became the first secretary of the United States Treasury. He was eventually killed in a duel with Aaron Burr.

Billie Holiday

Billie Holiday grew up in Baltimore. She moved to New York with her mother and made her jazz singing debut in Harlem nightclubs. She sang in various clubs and produced several records, helping form the foundation of American jazz.

Grace Hopper

Grace Hopper was born in New York City in 1906. She attended Vassar College in Poughkeepsie, New York. Hopper received a PhD in mathematics from Yale and became a rear admiral in the US Navy and a computer scientist. She helped program the first computers and developed software that made computers easier for others to program.

John Jay

John Jay was born in 1745 in New York. He served as a New York delegate to the First and Second Continental Congresses. George Washington nominated Jay to be the first chief justice of the Supreme Court. He also was the state of New York's first chief judge, helped draft the New York State Constitution, and was governor of New York from 1795 to 1801.

John Jay

Eugene O'Neill

Eugene O'Neill was born in 1888 in New York City. He wrote many plays about troubled individuals and families. He became a member of the Greenwich Village literary scene in Manhattan. He won four Pulitzer Prizes for Drama. O'Neill was the first American playwright to win a Nobel Prize for Literature.

Norman Rockwell

Norman Rockwell was born in New York City in 1894. He began art school at age fourteen. His long career produced many paintings and illustrations, including 322 paintings of everyday life for the cover of the *Saturday Evening Post*. He painted a famous version of Rosie the Riveter, a symbol of American women's wartime efforts.

Theodore Roosevelt

Theodore Roosevelt was the twenty-sixth president of the United States. He was born in Manhattan in 1858. He established numerous national parks, forests, and monuments to protect the nation's natural resources. He is one of the most famous and well-liked presidents in history, as well as the youngest.

New Yorkers walk down
the street in Buffalo.

3 Who Lives in New York?

New York is home to nearly twenty million people. This makes New York the fourth-largest state in the country. According to the 2010 US census, on average there are 411 people per square mile in the state. About 40 percent of New York's population lives in New York City.

The Entry Point

Beginning in the mid-1800s, New York City served as the main entry point for European immigrants into the United States for more than a century. It continues to be a major point of entry today. As a result, New York has become one of the most ethnically diverse states in the nation. Although the United States is often called the great American melting pot, it is probably more accurate to think of it as a giant tossed salad. People who come to America hold on to aspects of their culture and traditions even as they blend into American society. New York represents the same tossed salad on a smaller scale.

FAST FACT

According to a *New York Times* article, one in every 1,500 people born in New York State has his or her own Wikipedia page. The same data shows that New York City produces more famous journalists than any other place in the country.

Castle Garden served as an immigration center from 1855 to 1890.

Immigration to New York grew at a rapid pace in the nineteenth century. At first, immigrants entered at ports without any official processing or services. This left new immigrants vulnerable to scam artists. In 1855, the government opened Castle Garden, a former fort near the tip of Manhattan, as an immigration center. Immigrants paid a customs fee and had their luggage inspected before entering. Once inside Castle Garden, their name and other information was recorded. The government set up approved transit services, currency exchanges, and information exchanges. There was also a Labor Exchange that offered temporary employment. Castle Garden closed in 1890. In 1892, the Ellis Island immigrant processing center opened in New York Harbor.

From 1800 to 1880, the city's population increased dramatically each decade due to immigration. The immigrants of the mid-1800s came mostly from northern and western Europe, especially Germany and Ireland. Escaping poverty and **famine**, these men and women came in huge numbers. By 1850, nearly half the people living in New York City were foreign born.

New York's Biggest Colleges and Universities

(All enrollment numbers are from *US News and World Report* 2018 college rankings.)

1. New York University, New York City

(26,135 undergraduate students)

2. State University of New York (SUNY), University at Buffalo, Buffalo

(20,411 undergraduate students)

3. City College of New York (CUNY), New York City College of Technology, New York City

(17,282 undergraduate students)

4. SUNY, Stony Brook University, Stony Brook

(17,026 undergraduate students)

5. CUNY, Hunter College, New York City

(16,723 undergraduate students)

6. St. John's University, New York City

(16,440 undergraduate students)

7. CUNY, Queen's College, New York City

(16,326 undergraduate students)

8. Syracuse University, Syracuse

(15,218 undergraduate students)

9. CUNY, Baruch College, New York City

(15,210 undergraduate students)

10. Cornell University, Ithaca

(14,566 undergraduate students)

New York University

Hunter College

Cornell University

A Classic New York Bagel

New Yorkers take pride in many of their iconic foods, including a good New York City bagel. The bagels are prized for their deep flavor, chewy interior, and blistered crust. Many New Yorkers say you can't get a good bagel anywhere else in the country.

In New York, and especially New York City, bagels are often paired with lox. Lox is salmon that has been cured or brined (aged in salt or soaked in salt water) until it is very soft and almost see-through. Then it's thinly sliced.

Classic New York City Bagels with Lox:

Ingredients:

- 4 bagels, (preferably from New York City!)
- 8 slices of lox
- 1 tub of plain cream cheese
- 1 tablespoon of capers, rinsed
- ¼ of a red onion, thinly sliced
- Freshly chopped dill, if desired

Directions:

1. Slice the bagels and spread with cream cheese.
2. Place two slices of folded lox on top.
3. Sprinkle with a few capers and a few rings of red onion.
4. If desired, sprinkle with chopped dill.

In the 1880s, the city's population doubled when a new wave of immigration began. People from Italy, other southern European countries, and eastern Europe began coming to America in large numbers. They wanted to escape poverty and religious persecution. They were looking for economic opportunity and greater freedom. That wave of immigration continued through the early decades of the twentieth century. Starting in the late 1800s, the US government began limiting the number of immigrants admitted to the United States.

After these **restrictions** were eased in the late 1960s, New York again became the destination of choice for many immigrants. Two large waves of Russian Jews entered in the 1970s and 1990s, for example. But many of the new immigrants have come from places other than Europe, including Asia, Africa, the Caribbean, Central America, and Mexico. New York City is home to people of practically every religion and nationality in the world.

Upstate and Western New York

New York's cultural attractions are not limited to New York City. A state as big and diverse as New York has much to offer. Since 1863, historic Saratoga Springs has been home to a famous horseracing track. Saratoga is also where you will find the Saratoga Performing Arts Center. The center is the summer residence for the New York City Ballet and the Philadelphia Orchestra. Art lovers are sure to appreciate the Hyde Collection, which can be found in Glens Falls. This museum includes works by some of the finest European and American artists. The Bethel Woods Center for the Arts is a not-for-profit performing arts

FAST FACT
During and after World War II, **significant** numbers of black people from the rural South moved into northern and western cities, including New York City.

Today, Ellis Island is a museum that tells the stories of the immigrants who reached New York by boat.

Who Lives in New York? • 51

The Saratoga Race Course is a popular summer attraction in Upstate New York.

The National Baseball Hall of Fame and Museum hosts more than three hundred thousand visitors each year.

center and museum. It is located on the site of the famous 1969 Woodstock music festival. Today, visitors come to enjoy concerts in every musical genre. The quiet village of Cooperstown is home to the National Baseball Hall of Fame and Museum.

Throughout New York, there is beauty around every corner. The people of Buffalo are proud of the beautiful old stone houses with large porches that line their city streets. They are also proud of the Darwin D. Martin House, one of several homes in the area designed by world-famous architect Frank Lloyd Wright. Nearby, the majestic waterfalls of Niagara Falls remain a major tourist attraction. In Rochester, home to Xerox and Eastman Kodak, the citizens are pleased with their city's nickname: "The Image City of the World." Many citizens enjoy taking walks along the Erie Canal at night.

Rochester has a long history of social consciousness. Susan B. Anthony, who fought for women's voting rights, lived there. And Frederick Douglass, the African American leader of the movement to end slavery, lived in the city and is buried there.

Syracuse is home to the Great New York State Fair, a thirteen-day fair that marks the end of summer. Basketball lovers enjoy going to the Carrier Dome to root for the Syracuse Orange, Syracuse University's Division I basketball team.

The Albany area is home to the New York State Museum and several entertainment venues. These include the Palace Theatre, The Egg, the

Carmelo Kyam Anthony

Carmelo Kyam Anthony was born in Brooklyn and played college basketball at Syracuse. After playing for the Denver Nuggets and the New York Knicks, he was traded to the Oklahoma City Thunder in 2017. Anthony has played on the USA Olympic team four times.

Tony Bennett

Tony Bennett was born in Astoria, New York, in 1926. Today, he lives in New York City and is famous as a jazz, pop, and show tunes singer.

Billy Crystal

Actor Billy Crystal was born in Long Island in 1948. In addition to many starring roles, Crystal has lent his voice to a number of characters in animated films, such as Mike in *Monsters, Inc.*

Alicia Keys

Singer and pianist Alicia Keys was born in New York City in 1981. She often mentions the state of New York in her music. Beyond writing, producing, and recording music, Keys also works as an activist. She is the recipient of fifteen Grammy Awards.

Lady Gaga

Lady Gaga grew up in Manhattan. She is famous for her energetic songs and her wild costumes.

Lin-Manuel Miranda

Lin-Manuel Miranda is the composer, lyricist, and performer who created the musical *Hamilton*. *Hamilton* won the 2016 Pulitzer Prize in Drama and eleven Tony Awards. He lives in New York City.

New York's Celebrities

Carmelo Kyam Anthony

Lady Gaga

Lin-Manuel Miranda

Times Union Center, and Proctors in nearby Schenectady. Albany also hosts many festivals throughout the year, such as the Tulip Festival, PearlPalooza, and LarkFest.

Residents and visitors alike enjoy watching New York's many professional sports teams. Basketball fans can see the Knicks (National Basketball Association) or the Liberty (Women's National Basketball Association) play at Manhattan's Madison Square Garden, while the Nets play for the NBA in Brooklyn's Barclays Center. New York has three National Hockey League teams: the Buffalo Sabres, New York Islanders, and New York Rangers. It also has three National Football League teams—the Buffalo Bills, New York Giants, and New York Jets. (The last two actually play their home games across the Hudson River in New Jersey.) Both of New York's Major League Baseball teams got new stadiums in 2009. The New York Mets play at Citi Field in Queens. In their first year in a new Yankee Stadium in the Bronx, the New York Yankees won their twenty-seventh World Series. They are the most successful team in the history of Major League Baseball.

Strength in Diversity

One of the reasons New York is so unique is the big number of people who have immigrated to the United States through its ports. Many of these people have made their homes in New York City and the surrounding areas. New York State's citizens are known for their creativity and inventiveness. In fact, New York has patented more inventions per person since 1974 than any other state.

The Changing Face of New York

In 1790, New York had 340,120 people. By 2017, New York had an estimated 19,849,399 people. New York's population has generally always grown. Yet in recent decades it has either decreased slightly or evened out. It's estimated that between July 2015 and July 2016, New York State's population **declined** by about 1,900 people.

The decline in population is taking place mostly in the regions outside of New York City. These are Upstate New York, Western New York, and the Southern Tier. (Often all of these regions are called "Upstate.") In the 2016 US Census Bureau estimate, only five cities and seven upstate counties outside of the New York City metropolitan area grew in population since 2010. It is likely that the population decline is caused by the lack of jobs. Upstate New York's economy has been based on manufacturing. Today, manufacturing jobs are disappearing from the region. About 73,000 people left New York State in that 2015–2016 time period.

This map shows New York's counties.

The two upstate counties with the highest population growth were Saratoga County and Tompkins County. Saratoga County has a thriving technology scene. Tompkins County is where Cornell University is located. Meanwhile, downstate New York (the New York City metropolitan area) has generally continued to grow in population.

New York City is also losing residents to other parts of the country. However, in July 2016, New York City's population reached a new high of 8,537,673. (That number comes from US Census Bureau estimates.) New York City's growth is thanks to foreign immigration and high birth rates.

The shifts in population have a variety of effects. If New York's population growth doesn't keep up with that of other states, it will lose representatives in Congress. It will also lose electoral votes in presidential elections. That will mean the state, normally a national powerhouse, will have less of an influence in national politics. Population numbers can also impact how much money an area gets from the state and federal government. The languages people speak can be another interesting effect of population changes. For instance, 30 percent of New York's population has a first language that isn't English. The most common native language is Spanish.

Many people picture skyscrapers and Wall Street when they think about New York's economy. However, all kinds of industries bring money to the state. Here, a farmer tends to his fields.

4 At Work in New York

New York State is home to a wide range of industries. New York City is one of the great financial capitals of the world. It is also a capital of fashion, publishing, tourism, entertainment, and much more. Farther north and west of New York City, the state has manufacturing towns and a **significant** amount of agriculture.

The Foundation of New York's Economy

Much of the state's early success can be traced to its waterways. It has a key role in transportation and shipping. New York Harbor is one of the best natural harbors on the Atlantic coast. It is a deep and sheltered harbor. Large ships can enter easily. Even in the early 1800s, New York City was a major port. The opening of the Erie Canal in 1825 made it even better connected. The Erie Canal connected the city and its port with Western New York, the Great Lakes, and

FAST FACT

Wall Street is America's center of finance in New York City. It is named after a wall that once stood in the same location. Dutch settlers built a defensive wall against the English on the southern tip of Manhattan. The wall was never used to defend the Dutch, though. It no longer stands, but the street was named for the wall that once was.

A canoer enjoys the Cayuga-Seneca Canal, part of the New York State Canal System.

the Midwest. With later expansions, the current 524-mile (843 km) New York State Canal System links the Great Lakes to the Hudson River and five waterways in Canada. The trade route created by the canal system touches almost every major city in New York.

Today, New York is also crisscrossed by miles and miles of highways for moving products—and people—across the state. The Governor Thomas E. Dewey Thruway links New York City and Buffalo. It also has extensions that connect it to major highways in Massachusetts, Pennsylvania, New Jersey, and Connecticut. The 570-mile (917 km) road system is one of the longest toll-supported highway systems in the United States.

The state also has thousands of miles of commercial and passenger railroad tracks. The commercial lines carry freight. Passenger lines serving New York include Amtrak and two large commuter lines in the New York City area. These are the Metro-North Railroad and the Long Island Rail Road.

Drivers began traveling the first part of the Governor Thomas E. Dewey Thruway in 1954.

Millions of people need to get to and from their jobs in and around New York City each day. Many use one of the commuter railroads or the New York City subway system. The Long Island Rail Road is made up of 594 miles (956 km) of track. It's the busiest commuter railroad in the United States. It runs from the eastern tip of Long Island, through suburban Suffolk and Nassau Counties, and into Queens, Brooklyn, and Manhattan. Metro-North connects New

York City with its northern suburbs in Westchester and other counties and with northeastern suburbs in Connecticut. It is the second-busiest commuter line. This system is composed of 787 miles (1,267 km) of track. Additionally, the New York City subway system is the country's largest and busiest urban mass transit system.

The Long Island Rail Road is the busiest commuter railroad in the United States.

Aside from providing transportation, these transit systems provide jobs. Tens of thousands of New Yorkers work for the railroads and subway system. Tens of thousands of others work at New York's airports.

The transportation industry also includes trucking, bus and taxi service, and water transportation. New York State is home to five major seaports. The Port of Albany is located on the Hudson River. It connects to the New York State Canal System. From there, cargo can be carried by truck, rail, or air to its final destination. The Port of Buffalo is located at the eastern end

The Port of Albany as seen from the Port of Rensselaer

A Kodak Moment

George Eastman lived from 1854 to 1932.

This model of Kodak camera was manufactured in the early 1900s.

George Eastman was a twenty-four-year-old bank teller living in Rochester, New York, when he bought his first camera. The camera was heavy and expensive. Developing photos was also expensive, and it was a long, hard process. Eastman spent the next three years developing a better method. In 1880, he patented a new way to coat glass plates, the surface on which the image was exposed and developed. The next year, he launched the Eastman Dry Plate Company. Soon, he shifted from developing photos on glass plates to film. In 1884, the company became the Eastman Dry Plate and Film Company. In 1888, his company released its first camera, the Kodak.

The Kodak camera provided a simple new way to take a picture. The Kodak slogan was "You press the button, we do the rest." The camera came preloaded with film, and when it was full, the company developed the roll. Over time, the process grew so easy that anyone could do it. Soon, amateur camera clubs popped up and people across America were taking snapshots for family photo albums.

The company, now called the Eastman Kodak Company, also provided professional photofinishing and developed a special film that was an important step toward the birth of the motion picture industry. Kodak became the biggest name in photography in America. Any event worth recording was commonly referred to as "a Kodak moment."

After more than a century in business, Kodak filed for bankruptcy in 2012. Kodak had relied on selling film to consumers and the movie industry. Those sales dropped as digital technology took over. Kodak did develop a successful digital camera line and a photo printer dock, but they lost money on camera sales. Soon customers were using smartphones as cameras. Today, Kodak focuses on imaging and printing products and services for businesses.

of Lake Erie. It is the first major port of call for foreign goods entering the United States via the Great Lakes. The Port of Ogdensburg is the northernmost port in New York. It's the only US port on the Saint Lawrence Seaway. The Port of Oswego is located on Lake Ontario. The Port of New York and New Jersey, located in New York Harbor, is the largest port complex on the East Coast. In 2016, the port handled about $200 billion worth of cargo.

New York Industry

In the early 1940s, manufacturing industries employed 33.8 percent of working people in New York State. But by the beginning of the twenty-first century, just one in ten jobs in New York was in manufacturing. Manufacturing is no longer the backbone of the New York economy. However, manufacturing still has an important part to play. It is especially strong in certain areas of the state. Rochester, for example, is home to many manufacturing companies. Companies there produce photographic and copier equipment, scientific instruments, and more. Factories in Syracuse make paper products, telecommunications

The work done on the floor of the New York Stock Exchange is fast paced and important.

The Guggenheim Museum was designed by architect Frank Lloyd Wright.

The Hyde Collection Museum in Glens Falls

Today, the Vanderbilt Mansion is a National Historic Site.

equipment, and construction materials, among other goods.

As manufacturing declined, other parts of the state's economy grew. Today, more than one out of every five New York workers is employed in education or health care. This sector of the economy includes teachers, doctors, nurses, health-care technicians, therapists, and social workers. Many New Yorkers are also employed in retail trade. They sell everything from groceries to clothes to automobiles. These types of jobs can be found throughout the state. Certain industries are concentrated mainly in New York City. In fact, the city is known the world over as a leading center of banking and finance, publishing, fashion, and entertainment.

New York City is considered by many to be a cultural capital of the world. Tourism and entertainment contribute a significant amount to the state's economy. More than sixty million people visited New York City in 2016. This incredible number of visitors makes it the country's top tourist destination.

Visitors flock to Manhattan to see a Broadway play, attend an opera at the Metropolitan Opera House, or listen to the

The Finger Lakes region features many vineyards.

New York Philharmonic at David Geffen Hall. Many also come to visit New York's many famous museums, including the Metropolitan Museum of Art, the Museum of Modern Art, the American Museum of Natural History, and the Guggenheim.

Tourism is not limited to the city, however. In 2016, there were 239 million visitors to New York State. The Greater Niagara area boasts a world-class **symphony**, wonderful art collections, and, of course, Niagara Falls. The Catskill Mountains offer skiing, rock climbing, and hiking. The Hudson Valley region is home to many historic homes and mansions. These include Franklin D. Roosevelt's home and the Vanderbilt Mansion in Hyde Park. The Hudson Valley is also a great place to experience the Northeast's famous fall foliage. North of the Hudson Valley, Lake George and Lake Champlain offer visitors the opportunity to enjoy boating and water sports.

Staying Green

Agriculture is also important to the state's economy. New York is the second-largest

FAST FACT

In 2014, New York State banned large-scale hydraulic fracturing. This process is also known as "fracking." The technique is a way to get natural gas from the ground by injecting high-pressure liquid deep into the ground. However, fracking strains the environment. Increased earthquakes are often seen in the fracking area.

New Industries in New York

Rochester is home to cutting-edge technology.

While manufacturing jobs overall are declining in the state, there's a new trend in creating high-tech manufacturing jobs. One example of this trend is the opening of a new manufacturing facility in Rochester, New York. The American Institute for Manufacturing Integrated Photonics (AIM Photonics) is opening a testing, assembly, and packaging (TAP) facility. The facility is **funded** by the government. It gives AIM Photonics members shared access to expensive photonics research and development equipment. Members include businesses and universities.

Photonics is the science of using and controlling photons. Photons are the smallest unit of light. Photonic devices use light to power lasers and fiber optics. You probably use fiber optics every day. They help to transmit data through long-distance telephone lines and over the internet.

Electronic devices like computers and smartphones use the power of the electron to operate and process information. (Electrons are part of atoms. Atoms are the smallest unit of matter.) Photonic devices use the power of the photon instead. Photons travel faster than electrons. Replacing electrons with photons can produce cheaper, faster, and more energy-efficient devices.

AIM Photonics's TAP facility will focus on research related to defense and national security. They will also focus on research in the energy, health-care, communications, and manufacturing sectors.

The federal and state governments hope that AIM Photonics can help the economy around the Finger Lakes region. Their economy has seen significant declines in chemical manufacturing. AIM Photonics itself won't create a large number of jobs, though. The government hopes that the facility will draw other photonics companies that can grow and create new jobs. To help accomplish that goal, New York State promised $250 million to create the new facility. The United States Department of Defense pledged $110 million. Private supporters committed another $250 million to the project. The facility is located in a former Kodak building.

apple-producing state in the United States. The industry supports almost seven hundred orchards and accounts for close to twenty thousand jobs. New York is a leader in grape production. It ranks third in the nation behind California and Washington.

Cows roam a dairy farm in Upstate New York.

The state is also the third-leading producer of dairy products; in 2016, it produced about 14.8 billion pounds (6.7 billion kg) of milk.

The New Economy

At the end of the first decade of the twenty-first century, New York was feeling the effects of the severe economic **recession** that had begun by 2008. Many people lost jobs in the banking and finance industry. Hundreds of billions of dollars in assistance from the US government helped the financial industry recover. Workers in other fields were also hard hit by the recession. But New York still had one of its best resources: its people.

One reason New York recovered so well is the state's large, skilled workforce. Throughout the years, the people of New York have made the state an exciting place to live, work, and visit. The region is filled with talent and innovation. It continues to be a major economic leader in the United States and across the world.

FAST FACT

New York City is home to the five biggest publishing companies in North America. These publishing companies (Penguin Random House, Macmillan, HarperCollins, Hachette, and Simon and Schuster) are often called "The Big Five." Many writers dream of working with these companies.

Constructing the New York State Capitol
Building in Albany took thirty-two years!

5 Government

New York City might be the biggest and most famous city in New York State, but the state capital is actually 152 miles (245 km) north. New York's capital is Albany. Here, New York's state assembly and senate gather to make laws. The governor lives in the executive mansion in Albany. The New York State Court of Appeals, the state's highest court, is based in Albany too.

In 2018, New York was represented in the US Congress by two senators and twenty-seven members in the House of Representatives. Only California and Texas have more United States representatives than New York.

How New Yorkers Vote

New York State is one of the three strongest states for the Democratic Party in the United States. In the last forty years, the state has had just one Republican governor. In 2018, Democrats controlled the state assembly and the governorship. Both of New York's United States

The Executive Mansion is where the governor lives.

New York is represented in Washington by twenty-nine members of Congress.

senators were Democrats. So were two-thirds of the state's United States representatives.

The state had nearly 12.5 million registered voters in 2016. More than 5.8 million people had registered as supporters of the Democratic Party. More than half of those voters lived in New York City. Of the 2.8 million voters who had registered as supporters of the Republican Party, less than 18 percent lived in New York City. Upstate certainly leans more Republican than New York City. However, there are more registered Democrats than registered Republicans in Upstate. Additionally, large upstate cities such as Buffalo, Syracuse, Albany, and Rochester have Democratic mayors. One of the challenges of governing a state like New York is balancing the needs and wants of the residents of its cities with those in rural communities.

New York's State Government

Just like the federal government, New York's state government is divided into three branches. These are the executive, legislative, and judicial branches.

The Executive Branch

The chief executive officer of the state is the governor. New York's governor is elected to a four-year term. The governor is responsible for enforcing the state's laws, appointing judges, and drawing up the state government's budget. He or she also introduces legislation that might be made into laws.

New Yorkers vote in the 2016 presidential election.

The Legislative Branch

As in most other states (and the federal government), New York's legislature is divided into two houses. The senate has 63 members. The assembly has 150 members. All are elected to two-year terms. The legislature passes the state's laws and approves the government's budget. Legislators can pass a law by a simple majority vote in both houses. If the governor vetoes a measure passed by the legislature, a two-thirds vote in both houses is needed to override the veto and enact the law.

The Judicial Branch

Unlike most states, New York's highest court is called the court of appeals. It is made up of a chief judge and six associate judges. All are appointed to fourteen-year terms. These judges hear cases appealed from lower courts. (An appeal is the request for a higher court to reverse a lower court's decision.) Below the court of appeals are the four appellate divisions of the state supreme court. Those courts mostly hear appeals from

The senate chamber in the New York State Capitol Building

lower courts such as district and county courts. Their justices are appointed by the governor from those elected to the next lower court. For New York, this is the state supreme court. These justices are elected to fourteen-year terms. Most cases start in the supreme court.

From Bill to Law

As in any government, the senators and members of the assembly in Albany have to work together to solve problems. Members of different parties often disagree about the correct way to attack a problem. However, they are frequently faced with a choice: compromise or get nothing done. New York government is often all about compromise.

Until 2009, Republicans had a majority in the state senate for more than forty years. On the other hand, the state assembly had been under Democratic control since 1974. The senate majority leader and the speaker of the assembly (the leaders of the houses) have enormous power. These two people decide what is voted on in their houses, and they often negotiate directly with the governor. This way of operating has caused some critics to refer to New York government as three people in a room controlling what happens. Their influence is so enormous that when they and the governor agree to do something, it is almost certain to happen.

Of course, not all the power lies with the leaders of the two houses and the governor. The senate majority leader and the speaker of the assembly always need the votes of their members in the legislature to pass a bill. Most new bills start with a single senator or assembly member. The politician introduces his or her idea to one chamber of the legislature. The idea must be drafted as a bill in a special legislative form. Once a bill is introduced, it is referred to a standing committee for debate. At this point, the bill can be amended (added to or changed), rejected, or passed. If a majority of committee members support the new bill, the full senate or assembly can debate, amend, and vote on it. If the bill gets a majority vote, it is passed to the other legislative house. The other house will then debate it. Even if the bill is approved in the other house, its journey to becoming a law is not over yet. The senate and the assembly often pass different versions. These need to be ironed out in a conference committee.

When the two houses finally agree on the details and wording of the bill, they send it to the governor for signature. If the governor signs a bill or fails to sign it within ten days, it becomes a law. If the governor does not like the bill, he or she can veto (or reject) it. (If the legislature is not in session, the governor has thirty days to decide. Failure to act equals a veto.) Both houses of the legislature then must pass the bill again by a two-thirds vote to override a veto and make the bill a law. If they do not, then the bill dies.

In many other states, a supreme court is the higest court. New York does have a state supreme court (pictured above), but the court of appeals is New York's highest court.

Education

New York is home to a variety of public and private schools. From kindergarten and elementary school all the way to college, the state provides many opportunities for learning. However, quality education requires money for teachers and supplies. **Funding** for education is a major issue for state voters and legislators. About 2.5 million students attend K–12 public schools in New York State. A major concern of many New Yorkers is the quality of public education.

For years, many New Yorkers complained that public schools were not getting enough funding from the state. Others saw problems with the way that funding was given out. In 1993,

George Pataki served as New York's governor from 1995 to 2007.

an organization called the Campaign for Fiscal Equity filed a lawsuit against the state of New York. They claimed that New York City schools weren't getting enough funds. They said city students were denied their right to a quality education. Early in 2001, Judge Leland DeGrasse of the state supreme court ruled that the state's formula for dividing up money unfairly and negatively impacted city students.

Judge DeGrasse ruled that the state had to come up with ways to give more money to New York City schools. George Pataki, then the governor of New York, fought the ruling for years. In 2007, a new governor took office, and state funding for New York City schools was increased. As a result of the 2008 recession, the promised funding was never fully delivered, though. New lawsuits have been filed to continue the fight for New York City schools.

Some residents of wealthy communities have a different complaint. They feel that the state's testing requirements are unfair. They think that only students in school districts that are doing poorly should need to pass a series of exams before heading to high school.

In 2009, the most important concern became the amount of money available for public education. The whole US economy was in a severe recession. Because of the hard economic times, governments around the country brought in fewer tax dollars. They had less money to spend. New York then had to make cuts in funding for public schools.

Also affected by the budget crisis was the State University of New York (SUNY). SUNY has more than six hundred thousand enrolled students and sixty-four campuses. It is one of the largest state university systems in the country. After state funding for SUNY was reduced, the university raised the tuition that

Social Media

Ask an adult to show you the official Twitter and Facebook accounts of the New York State Senate and New York State Assembly using the links below:

New York State Senate Social Media:
https://twitter.com/nysenate
https://www.facebook.com/NYsenate

New York State Assembly Majority Social Media:
https://twitter.com/NYSA_Majority
https://www.facebook.com/NYSAssemblyMajority

Find Your Representatives

It's easy to see who your New York State representatives are.

To find your New York State Senate representative, go to https://www.nysenate.gov/find-my-senator and enter in your address.

To find your New York State Assembly member, go to http://nyassembly.gov/mem/search and enter in your address.

Email Your Representatives

Once you have found your representatives, you can send them an email. Share your ideas for new legislation. You can also share your concerns about life in New York State and urge them to act on issues that are important to you.

Once you have found your senator using the steps outlined above, contact your state senator by clicking "Message Senator" on their result page.

Contact your state assembly member by clicking on the Contact Me button. Their email address will be listed on the Contact Information page.

Getting Involved Online

it charges students. However, in 2017, a plan was announced that allows many students to attend CUNY or SUNY schools tuition-free. The program is called the Excelsior Scholarship. Students from New York whose families make less than $125,000 per year and attend a two- or four-year college program qualify.

Recently, parents and teachers across the state began voicing their concern over the Common Core. Common Core is set of standards that detail what students are supposed to know at the end of each grade. Many parents and teachers feel that Common Core includes too many tests. They believe the teaching pace is too fast and it hurts children who need extra help in school.

It's important to stay up-to-date on issues that are happening in the state government. The state's legislature, governor, and judges make decisions that impact everyday life. This is shown in the debates around education, which impact every student in New York from preschool up through college.

As a resident of New York State, you can impact the government by educating yourself on issues. Contact your representatives. Speak out on the issues that matter to you. The entire state benefits when more voices are represented.

Glossary

American Civil War	A war in the United States between the North (Union) and the South (Confederates) that took place between 1861 and 1865.
confederacy	A group of people brought together for a common interest or goal.
convention	A meeting of persons for a common purpose.
decline	To go down in number; decrease.
devastating	Reducing to ruin.
diverse	Having variety.
famine	A great shortage of food.
fragrant	Having a nice scent.
funded	To get money from.
funding	Money to do something.
immigrants	People who come to a country to live there.
legislature	A body of persons having the power to make laws.
persecution	The act of being treated continually in a way meant to be cruel or harmful.
populous	Having a lot of people who live in a given place.
raid	A sudden attack.
recession	When the economy declines for a certain length of time.
restrictions	Things that are kept within bounds.
significant	Having much importance or a sizable presence.
strategic	Of great importance within a whole or for a planned purpose.
suffrage	The right to vote.
symphony	A large group of musicians who play wind, string, and percussion instruments; an orchestra.

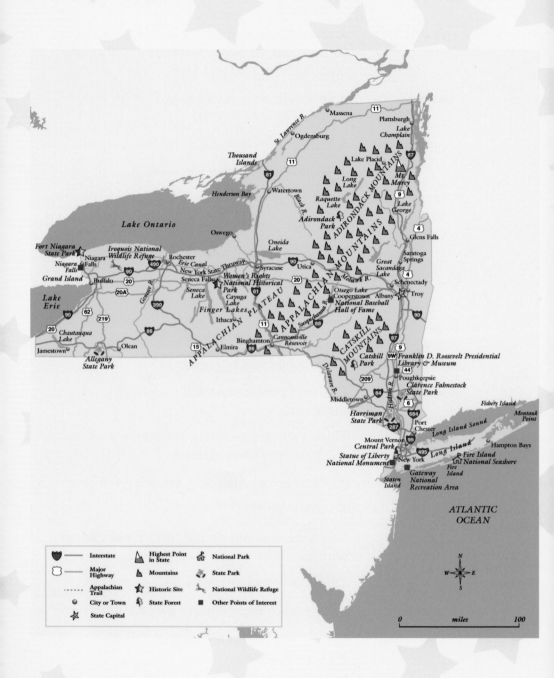

Map Labels

Massena
Plattsburgh
Lake Champlain
Ogdensburg
St. Lawrence R.
Thousand Islands
Lake Placid
Mt. Marcy
ADIRONDACK MOUNTAINS
Long Lake
Henderson Bay
Watertown
Raquette Lake
Adirondack Park
Lake George
Black R.
Glens Falls
Oswego
Oneida Lake
Great Sacandaga Lake
Saratoga Springs
Fort Niagara State Park
Niagara Falls
Iroquois National Wildlife Refuge
Rochester
Erie Canal
New York State Thruway
Syracuse
Utica
Mohawk R.
Schenectady
Niagara Falls
Grand Island
Buffalo
Seneca Falls
Women's Rights National Historical Park
Seneca Lake
Cayuga Lake
Otsego Lake
Cooperstown
National Baseball Hall of Fame
Albany
Troy
Lake Erie
Genesee R.
Finger Lakes
APPALACHIAN PLATEAU
APPALACHIAN MOUNTAINS
Susquehanna R.
Chautauqua Lake
Ithaca
Jamestown
Olean
Elmira
Binghamton
Cannonsville Reservoir
CATSKILL MOUNTAINS
Catskill Park
Franklin D. Roosevelt Presidential Library & Museum
Allegany State Park
Delaware R.
Middletown
Clarence Fahnestock State Park
Harriman State Park
Poughkeepsie
Port Chester
Fishers Island
Montauk Point
Hudson R.
Long Island Sound
Mount Vernon
Central Park
Statue of Liberty National Monument
New York
Long Island
Hampton Bays
Fire Island
Fire Island National Seashore
Staten Island
Gateway National Recreation Area
ATLANTIC OCEAN

Legend

- Interstate
- Major Highway
- Appalachian Trail
- City or Town
- State Capital
- Highest Point in State
- Mountains
- Historic Site
- State Forest
- National Park
- State Park
- National Wildlife Refuge
- Other Points of Interest

N W E S

0 miles 100

Map Skills

1. What's the westernmost lake that borders New York?

2. What wildlife refuge is south of Lake Ontario?

3. What ocean touches New York's border?

4. Ogdensburg is closest to what river?

5. What city is northeast of the state capital?

6. Where is Fire Island National Seashore?

7. What is the highest point in the state?

8. What highway crosses the state east to west?

9. What point of interest is due east of the Catskill Mountains?

10. What is the easternmost city or town on this map?

Answers:

1. Lake Erie
2. The Iroquois National Wildlife Refuge
3. The Atlantic Ocean
4. The Saint Lawrence River
5. Troy
6. Long Island
7. Mount Marcy5
8. Highway 90
9. The Franklin D. Roosevelt Presidential Library and Museum
10. Hampton Bays

Further Information

Books

Berman, Eleanor, Lee Magill, and AnneLise Sorensen. *DK Eyewitness Travel Family Guide: New York City*. Revised edition. New York: DK, 2016.

Crane, Cody. *My United States: New York*. New York: Scholastic, 2017.

Faust, Daniel R., and Amelie von Zumbusch. *The First Peoples of New York*. New York: PowerKids Press, 2015.

Websites

New York State Department of State: Fun and Facts Kid's Room
https://www.dos.ny.gov/kids_room/508/home2.html
Learn more about the history of New York, view pictures, and explore links.

New York State Museum
http://www.nysm.nysed.gov
Browse photos of exciting exhibits, including minerals and Native American artifacts.

Official New York State Tourism Website
http://iloveny.com
Explore each region of New York State and find upcoming events.

Official Website of New York State
http://www.ny.gov
Find facts about New York's state government, including information about the agencies that help run New York.

Index